How Could You?

Kids Talk About Trust

Written by
Nancy Loewen

Illustrated by
Omarr Wesley

Content Advisor: Lorraine O. Moore, Ph.D., Educational Psychology

Reading Advisor: Lauren A. Liang, M.A., Literacy Education, University of Minnesota

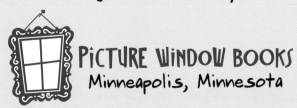

PICTURE WINDOW BOOKS
Minneapolis, Minnesota

Editor: Nadia Higgins
Designer: Thomas Emery
Page production: Picture Window Books
The illustrations in this book were prepared digitally.

Picture Window Books
5115 Excelsior Boulevard
Suite 232
Minneapolis, MN 55416
1-877-845-8392
www.picturewindowbooks.com

Printed in the United States of America.

Library of Congress Cataloging-in-Publication Data
Loewen, Nancy, 1964–
  How could you? : kids talk about trust / written by Nancy Loewen ;
illustrated by Omarr Wesley.
    p. cm. Includes index.
  Summary: Uses an advice-column format to define trust and provide examples in
daily life.
  ISBN 1-4048-0031-X (library binding : alk. paper) 1. Trust—Juvenile
literature. [1. Trust.]
I. Wesley, Omarr, ill. II. Title.
  BJ1500.T78 L64 2003
  179'.9—dc21
                                                              2002005892

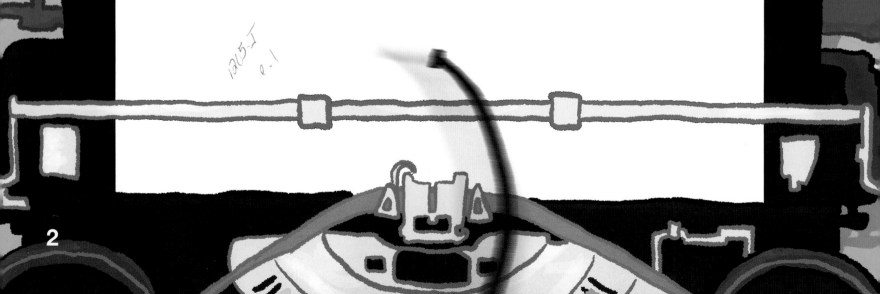

To my children,
Louis and Helena—
always my best teachers

3

Hi! My name is Frank B. Wize. Welcome to my very own advice column. I'll answer any question you throw at me. Except, I'm not so great at math. And I can never remember how many toes an iguana has. But I have lots to say about other things, like what to do if you get a really bad haircut and how to hold a really nice funeral for a dead hamster.

You might want to know how I, a 13-year-old, got to know so much about life. Well, I'm not a genius or anything. But you learn from your mistakes, right? When I was a little kid, I made LOTS of mistakes. Like once I stole the whole bag of CrazyNut bars that my friend was going to hand out to the class for his birthday. Another time, I wanted the new Galaxy Adventure game so badly that I held my breath until I passed out, right there in Computer Hut.

But I'm older now, and WIZER (get it?), and I'm starting to figure things out.

Today's column is about trust. You know, having other people believe you and being able to believe them. Making sure that what you SAY and what you DO are the same thing. So go ahead. Send in your letters. I'll be waiting to hear from you.

Sincerely,

Frank B. Wize

6

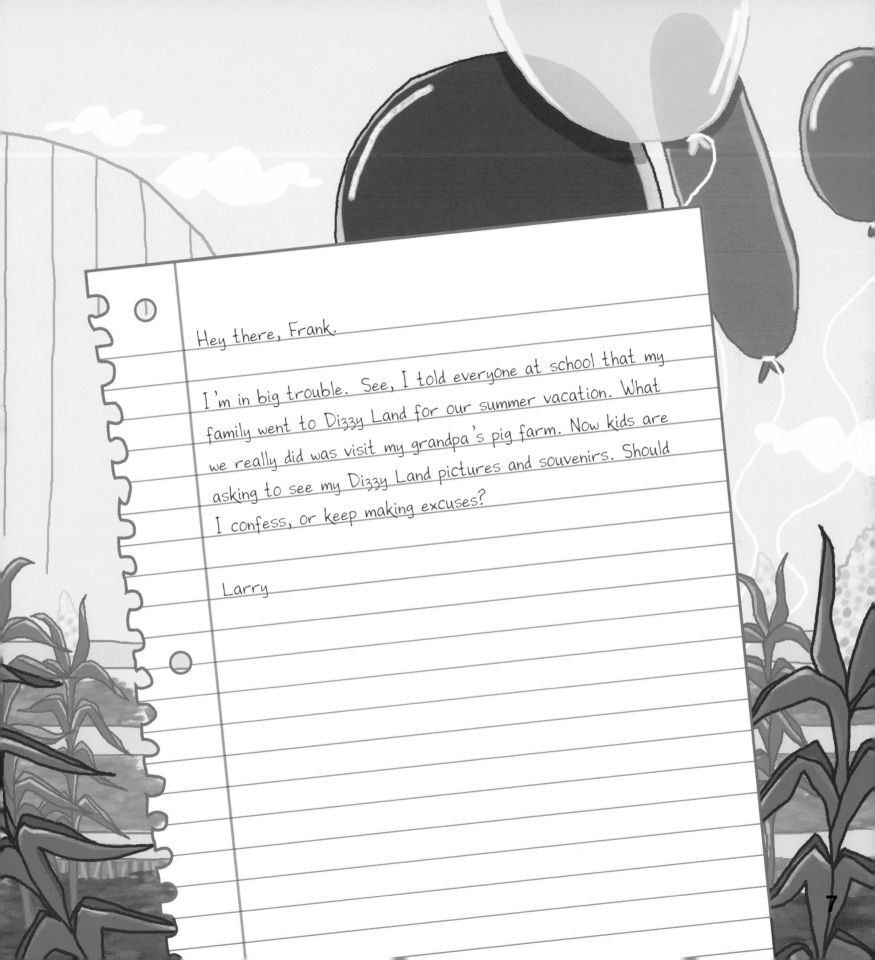

Hey there, Frank.

I'm in big trouble. See, I told everyone at school that my family went to Dizzy Land for our summer vacation. What we really did was visit my grandpa's pig farm. Now kids are asking to see my Dizzy Land pictures and souvenirs. Should I confess, or keep making excuses?

Larry

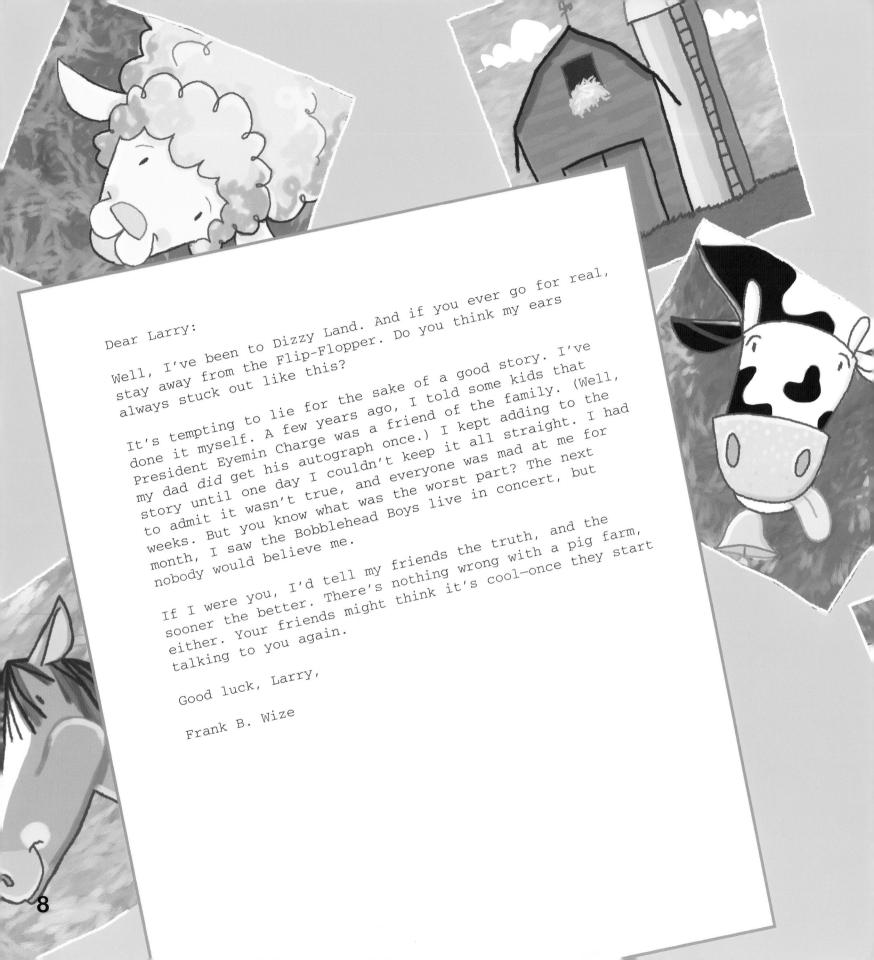

Dear Larry:

Well, I've been to Dizzy Land. And if you ever go for real, stay away from the Flip-Flopper. Do you think my ears always stuck out like this?

It's tempting to lie for the sake of a good story. I've done it myself. A few years ago, I told some kids that President Eyemin Charge was a friend of the family. (Well, my dad *did* get his autograph once.) I kept adding to the story until one day I couldn't keep it all straight. I had to admit it wasn't true, and everyone was mad at me for weeks. But you know what was the worst part? The next month, I saw the Bobblehead Boys live in concert, but nobody would believe me.

If I were you, I'd tell my friends the truth, and the sooner the better. There's nothing wrong with a pig farm, either. Your friends might think it's cool—once they start talking to you again.

Good luck, Larry,

Frank B. Wize

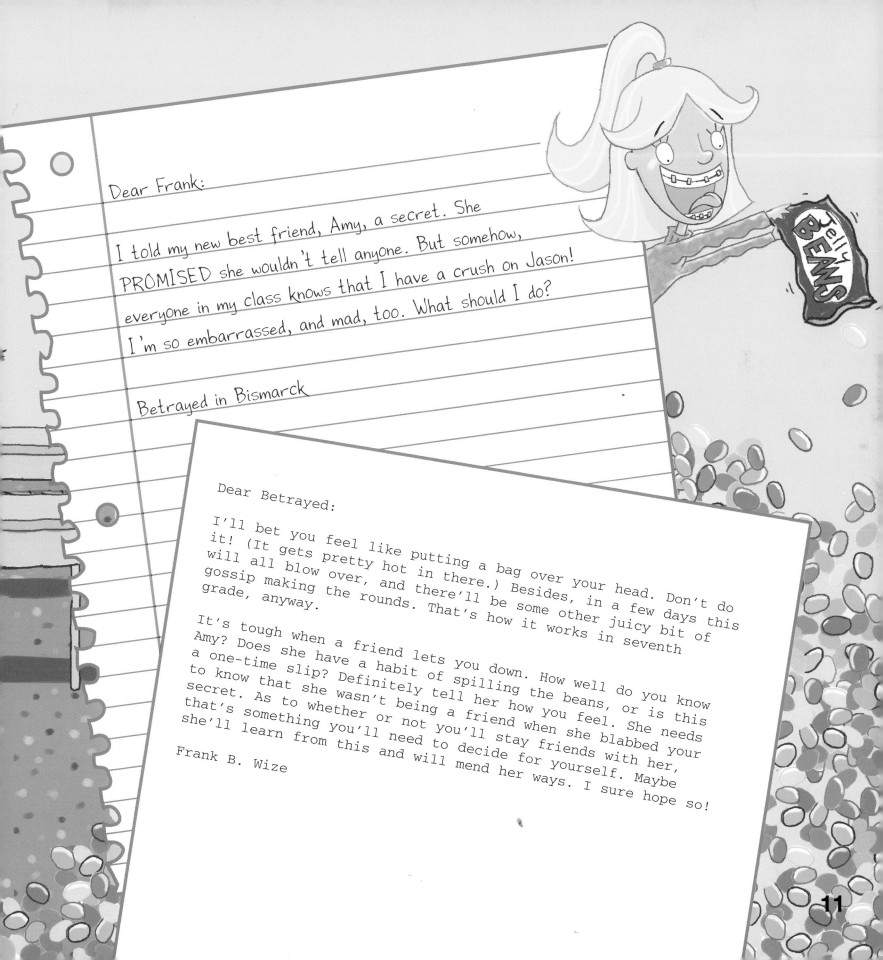

Dear Frank:

I told my new best friend, Amy, a secret. She PROMISED she wouldn't tell anyone. But somehow, everyone in my class knows that I have a crush on Jason! I'm so embarrassed, and mad, too. What should I do?

Betrayed in Bismarck

Dear Betrayed:

I'll bet you feel like putting a bag over your head. Don't do it! (It gets pretty hot in there.) Besides, in a few days this will all blow over, and there'll be some other juicy bit of gossip making the rounds. That's how it works in seventh grade, anyway.

It's tough when a friend lets you down. How well do you know Amy? Does she have a habit of spilling the beans, or is this a one-time slip? Definitely tell her how you feel. She needs to know that she wasn't being a friend when she blabbed your secret. As to whether or not you'll stay friends with her, that's something you'll need to decide for yourself. Maybe she'll learn from this and will mend her ways. I sure hope so!

Frank B. Wize

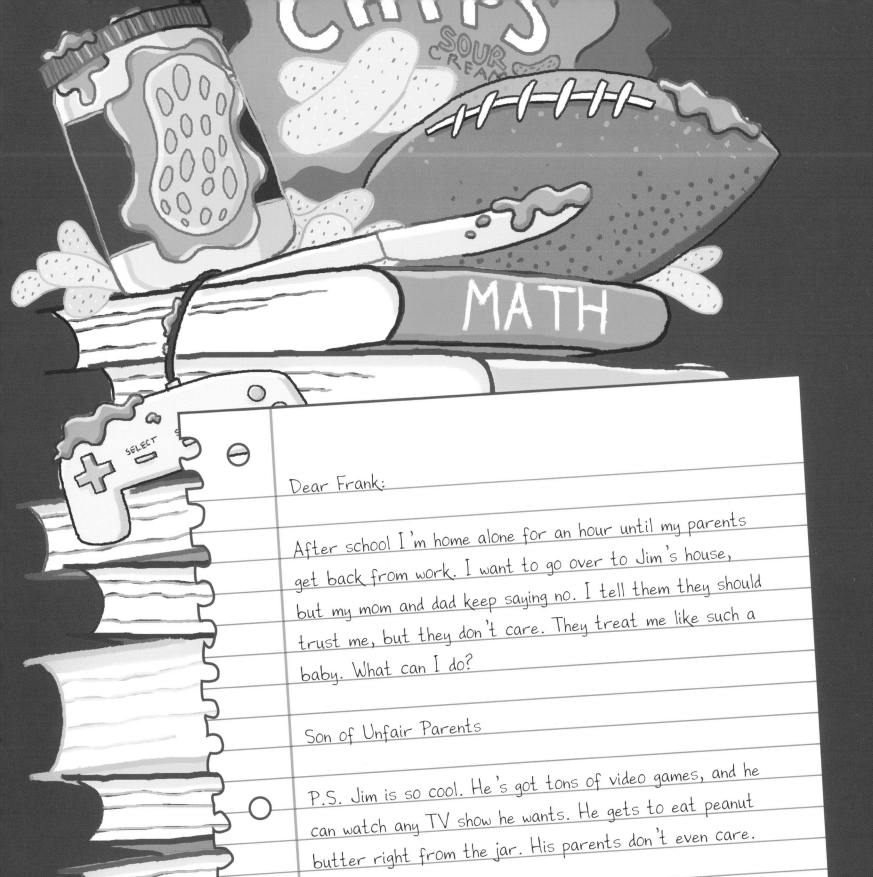

Dear Frank:

After school I'm home alone for an hour until my parents get back from work. I want to go over to Jim's house, but my mom and dad keep saying no. I tell them they should trust me, but they don't care. They treat me like such a baby. What can I do?

Son of Unfair Parents

P.S. Jim is so cool. He's got tons of video games, and he can watch any TV show he wants. He gets to eat peanut butter right from the jar. His parents don't even care.

Dear Son:

I can see why you'd want to go to Jim's house. You're probably thinking he has all the fun and you're stuck with all the rules.

But living without rules isn't all that great. I had a friend kind of like Jim. One afternoon at his house we ate a whole bag of Crumbly Crunchies (the cheesy kind) and drank a whole pitcher of grape juice. I threw up into their potted palm AND my hands were orange for three days. I was so sick that night I missed a double episode of *Star Enterprise*.

I hate to break it to you, but I don't think you'll get your way on this one, at least not yet. You can still be friends with Jim, though. Why don't you invite him to your house when your parents are around? Who knows? If your parents get to know Jim better, they might change their mind.

Frank B. Wize

P.S. My parents STILL treat me like a kid. But you know something? Even when I don't like their rules, it is kind of nice to know that they care so much.

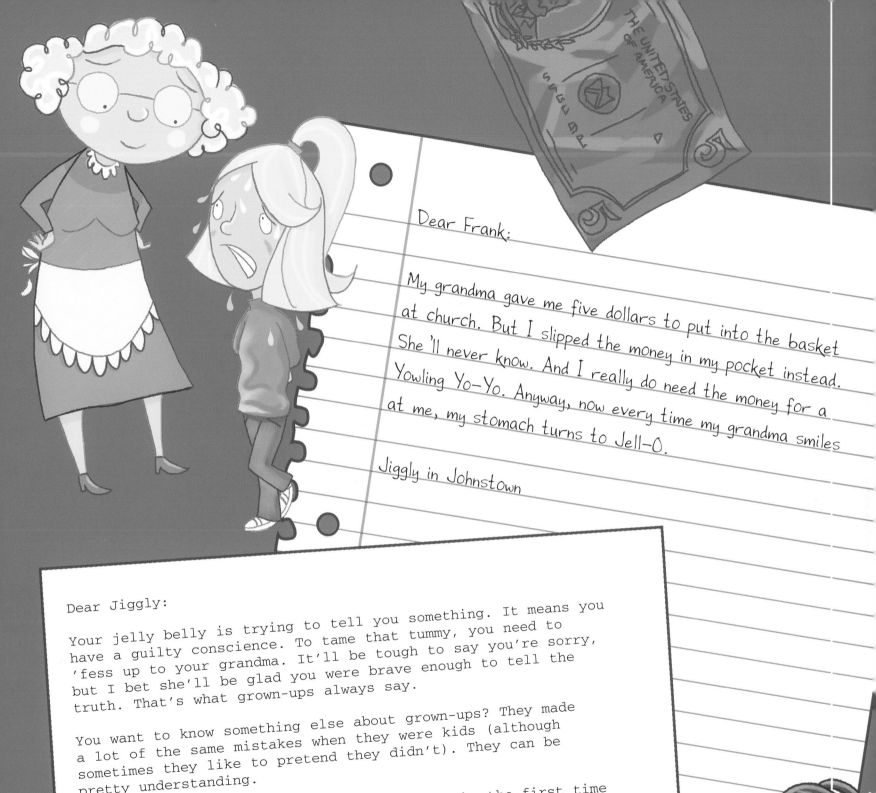

Dear Frank:

My grandma gave me five dollars to put into the basket at church. But I slipped the money in my pocket instead. She'll never know. And I really do need the money for a Yowling Yo-Yo. Anyway, now every time my grandma smiles at me, my stomach turns to Jell-O.

Jiggly in Johnstown

Dear Jiggly:

Your jelly belly is trying to tell you something. It means you have a guilty conscience. To tame that tummy, you need to 'fess up to your grandma. It'll be tough to say you're sorry, but I bet she'll be glad you were brave enough to tell the truth. That's what grown-ups always say.

You want to know something else about grown-ups? They made a lot of the same mistakes when they were kids (although sometimes they like to pretend they didn't). They can be pretty understanding.

Another word of advice: My Yowling Yo-Yo broke the first time I used it. Come to think of it, so did my brother's. Just thought you should know.

Frank B. Wize

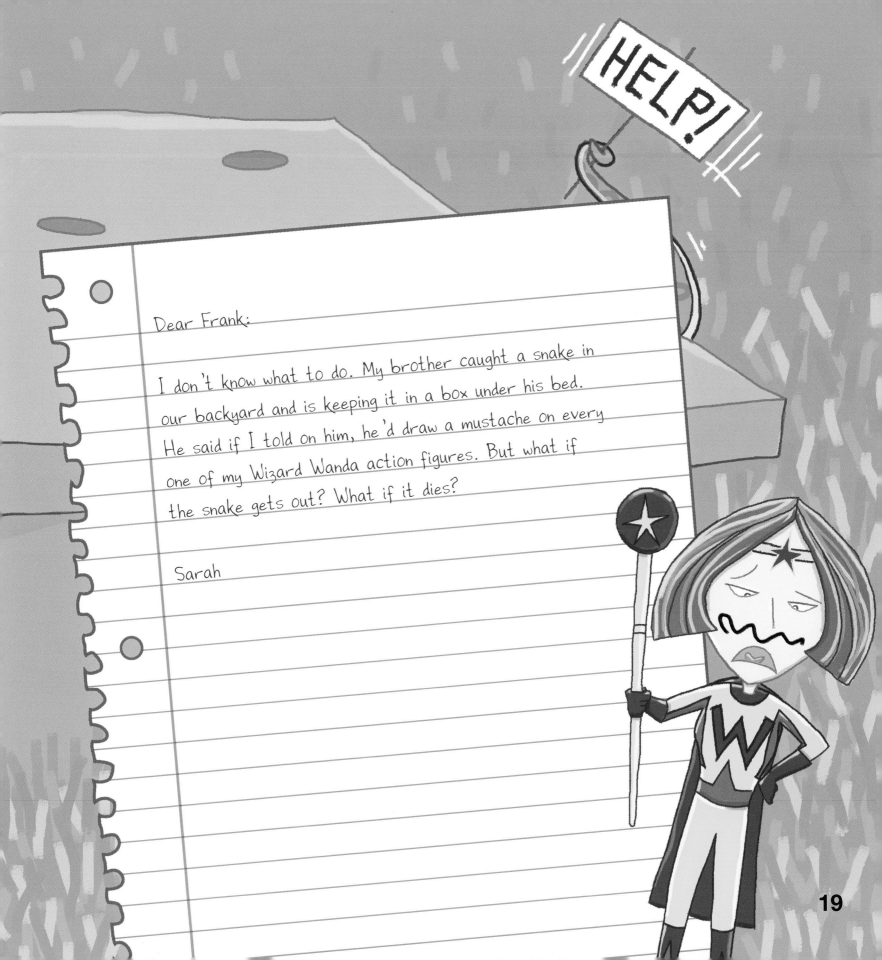

Dear Frank:

I don't know what to do. My brother caught a snake in our backyard and is keeping it in a box under his bed. He said if I told on him, he'd draw a mustache on every one of my Wizard Wanda action figures. But what if the snake gets out? What if it dies?

Sarah

Dear Sarah:

Let's do some imagining here. What would happen if your mom found a snake in the dirty laundry? What would happen if your dad found a dead snake under the bed? What would happen if the snake got under the oven?

I don't like what I'm seeing, and I bet you don't, either. In my opinion, this is a secret that needs to be told—for the sake of the snake, if not your brother. Try talking to your brother one more time. If he won't set the snake free himself, then you'll just have to tell your parents. In the meantime, find a safe place for your Wizard Wandas.

For all my readers, here's something I've learned about secrets. Some secrets are okay to keep, but others aren't. How do you tell the difference? If someone (or some snake) needs help, or if someone is doing something dangerous, then it's a good idea to tell a grown-up. Sometimes you just have to step back and look at the big picture. What would happen if you told someone the secret? What would happen if you DIDN'T?

And by the way, snakes don't like cat food. Don't ask me how I know.

Frank B. Wize

Dear Eagle Eyes:

Let me be frank. (Ha! I'm already Frank. Frank, frank—get it?) Anyway, what you're doing has a name. It's called cheating. Doesn't sound too good, does it?

In my old neighborhood, there was this kid who was always cheating. When we played kickball, he called fair balls foul. He copied other kids' book reports. No one wanted to play cards or board games with him, either, because they knew he would find a way to win. After a while, the kids started calling him Cheatin' Charlie, and they avoided him. I kind of felt sorry for him because he seemed lonely.

You don't want to go that way, Eagle Eyes. Cheating might get you something in the short term, but if you get in the habit of it, it's not a pretty scene. I think you should do your own work and be proud that it IS your work. Use those sharp eyes of yours for something else, like finding loose change on the sidewalk. That's just my two cents.

Frank B. Wize

23

Hi, Frank.

My mom got remarried recently, so now I've got a stepdad and a stepsister. They're okay, I guess, but my home doesn't feel like home anymore. Do you have any advice for me?

Feeling Stepped On

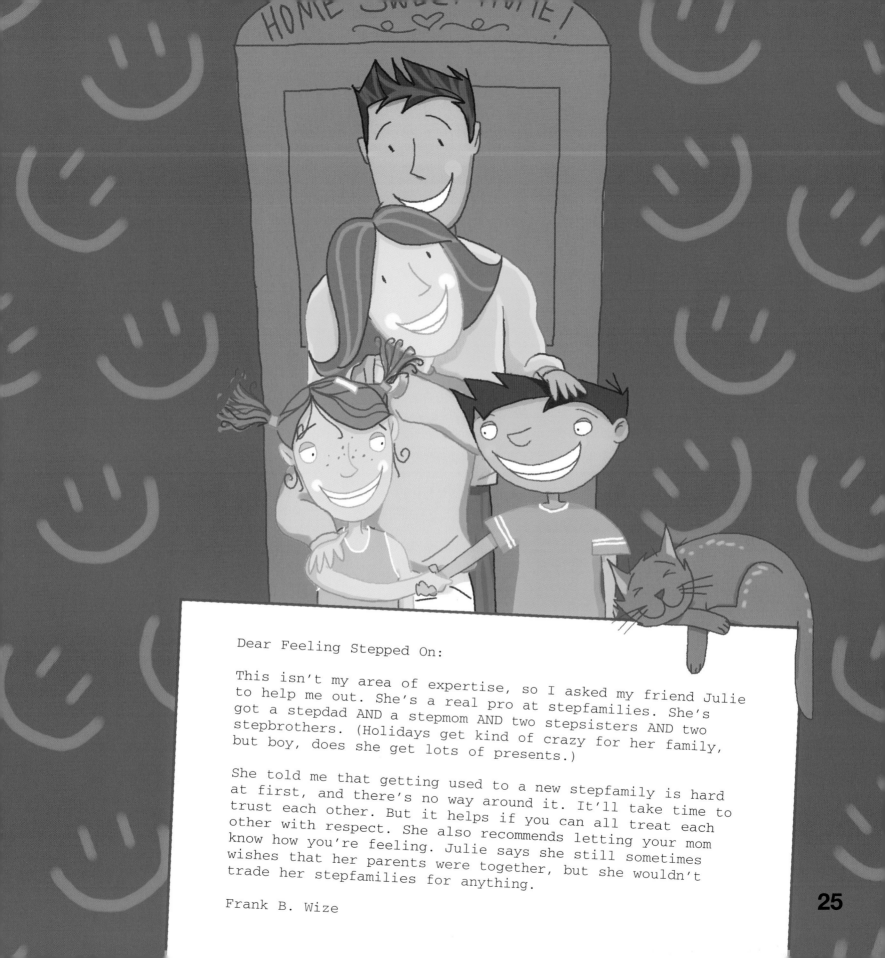

Dear Feeling Stepped On:

This isn't my area of expertise, so I asked my friend Julie to help me out. She's a real pro at stepfamilies. She's got a stepdad AND a stepmom AND two stepsisters AND two stepbrothers. (Holidays get kind of crazy for her family, but boy, does she get lots of presents.)

She told me that getting used to a new stepfamily is hard at first, and there's no way around it. It'll take time to trust each other. But it helps if you can all treat each other with respect. She also recommends letting your mom know how you're feeling. Julie says she still sometimes wishes that her parents were together, but she wouldn't trade her stepfamilies for anything.

Frank B. Wize

Dear Frank:

I'm not sure I like my aunt anymore. She keeps saying she'll take me to the museum, but she never does. She promised she'd come to my basketball game, but then she didn't show up. She gave me my birthday present two weeks late. Why is this happening?

Mad and Sad in Tennessee

Dear Mad and Sad:

I don't know your aunt, so I can only guess. Maybe she's swamped at work, or her love life's a mess, or maybe she's a secret spy. Another possibility is that your aunt is one of those people who makes promises too easily. They mean well, but they're not very reliable. My friend Alex is like that. When we make plans to meet at the park, half the time he's a no show. It could drive a kid crazy.

Try telling your aunt that her broken promises bother you and see if that helps. It worked for me, after my uncle forgot to come to my school play once. He felt so bad about it, he took me to a movie to make up for it.

To all my readers: If you say you're going to do something, do you do it? Do you keep your promises? It's something to think about.

Well, that's it for today's column. Thanks for sending me your questions about trust. I hope I've given you something to think about.

Good luck, and stay in touch!

Frank B. Wize

P.S. Keep reading for more good stuff ahead.

It's Quiz Time!

Take this fun quiz and find out how much you've learned about trust. Don't worry. It's nothing like the quizzes you take at school.

1. **If you get caught in a lie (or even if no one catches you), you should:**

   A. tell some more lies to cover it up.
   B. go live in a cave.
   C. tell the truth and say you're sorry.

2. **Grown-ups make rules because:**

   A. they're really aliens and are following orders from their leaders.
   B. they don't want kids to have any fun.
   C. they want kids to stay safe, learn a lot, and be happy.

3. **You know you can trust someone when:**

   A. you've got the same birthday.
   B. you've spent a lot of time with that person and you know he or she is honest and reliable.
   C. he or she has more toys than you do.

4. **The "big picture" is:**

   A. hanging in a museum in Paris.
   B. considering the whole situation, not just a part of it.
   C. the view from a space shuttle.

5. **If you do something you know is wrong, you will probably get:**

   A. warts.
   B. a puppy.
   C. a guilty conscience.

6. It's okay to tell a secret when:

    A. you're trying to get your brother or sister in trouble.
    B. aliens suck it out of your head.
    C. someone really needs help.

7. To get someone to trust you, you should:

    A. sit on them.
    B. be honest and reliable.
    C. buy them all the candy they can eat.

8. If your mom or dad remarries, you should:

    A. run away and join the circus.
    B. take a vow of silence.
    C. be respectful and give yourself time to feel comfortable with your new family.

9. Cheating:

    A. makes you smarter and more popular.
    B. will put hair on your chest.
    C. is bad news in the long run.

10. If someone lets you down, you should:

    A. tell them it bothers you.
    B. send them a bill.
    C. stick a pin in a voodoo doll.

Answer Key:

1-C, 2-C, 3-B, 4-B, 5-C, 6-C, 7-B, 8-C, 9-C, 10-A

From My Personal Hero File: Sacagawea

Have you seen a gold U.S. dollar coin? It's got a picture of a woman who's FAMOUS for being trustworthy. Sacagawea (sak-uh-juh-WEE-uh) was a Shoshone Indian who helped guide the famous Lewis and Clark expedition from 1804 to 1806. Here, take a look at this report:

Upon President Thomas Jefferson's request, Meriwether Lewis and William Clark set out to explore and map out the western territories—the land that lay between the Mississippi River and the Pacific Ocean. They asked Sacagawea and her husband, a French-Canadian fur trader, to be part of the team. Sacagawea was still a teenager at the time, and the mother of a baby boy. She was the only woman in the 33-member expedition.

Sacagawea helped out on the trip in many ways. Riding on horseback with her baby strapped to her back, Sacagawea pointed out landmarks. She knew what plants and berries were good to eat and which ones could be used for medicine. Once, on a boat during a storm, she saved some valuable papers and supplies from being lost overboard. She and her husband helped Lewis and Clark to communicate with the different Indian groups they met. Many of the Indians had never seen white people before and were prepared to defend their land. Because women and babies didn't usually travel with war parties, Sacagawea's presence let them know that this was a peaceful group.

Lewis and Clark trusted Sacagawea. They believed her and valued her opinions. She helped make the expedition a big success. Today, two whole centuries later, her story lives on. Neat, huh?

Words to Know

Here's a list of cool words and expressions I put together. It'll help you remember all the stuff we talked about.

advice—suggestions about what someone else should do. (It's okay to give advice when someone asks for it. But if you give advice without being asked, people might think you're being bossy. If someone says, "I don't remember asking for your advice," you'd better back off.)

big picture—Well, the biggest picture I've ever seen covered the side of an entire building. But what "the big picture" really means is to think about all the parts of a situation. Who are all the people involved? What are the different choices that could be made? What are some of the things that could happen?

expertise—a lot of knowledge about a certain subject. An "expert" is someone with "expertise." (Try saying that ten times fast.)

gossip—to talk about other people and their private, personal business. People who gossip a lot aren't exactly trustworthy, are they?

guilty conscience—that bad feeling inside you that says you did something wrong

respect—to have a high opinion of someone. To take that person seriously and treat them nicely.

rules—"official" instructions that tell you what to do and what not to do. Rules are a part of life, even for grown-ups. Without rules, life would be a whole lot more messy and complicated. Imagine what would happen if everybody ran red lights all the time. See what I mean?

spill the beans—I did this once in the grocery store. Boy, was my mom mad! But really, this is an expression that means to tell a secret.

trust—to depend on people, to believe that people will be honest and do what they say they're going to do. If you trust someone, you believe them and believe IN them.

To Learn More

At the Library

Casanova, Mary. *Stealing Thunder.* New York: Hyperion Books for Children, 1999.

Gantos, Jack. *Practice Makes Perfect for Rotten Ralph.* New York: Farrar, Straus & Giroux, 2002.

Havill, Juanita. *Jamaica and the Substitute Teacher.* Boston: Houghton Mifflin, 1999.

Peters, Julie Anne. *A Snitch in the Snob Squad.* Boston: Little, Brown & Company, 2001.

Raatma, Lucia. *Honesty.* Mankato, Minn.: Bridgestone Books, 2000.

On the Web

KidsHealth
http://www.kidshealth.org/kid
For answers to kids' common questions about growing up

FirstGov
http://www.kids.gov
For links to hundreds of kid-friendly government sites

Want to learn more about trust? Visit FACT HOUND at *http://www.facthound.com.*

Index